Anonymous

The State of the Representation of England and Wales

Delivered to the Society, the Friends of the People, associated for the

purpose of obtaining a parliamentary reform, on Saturday the 9th of

February 1793

Anonymous

The State of the Representation of England and Wales
Delivered to the Society, the Friends of the People, associated for the purpose of obtaining a parliamentary reform, on Saturday the 9th of February 1793

ISBN/EAN: 9783337331498

Printed in Europe, USA, Canada, Australia, Japan

Cover: Foto ©Suzi / pixelio.de

More available books at **www.hansebooks.com**

THE

STATE

OF THE

REPRESENTATION

OF

ENGLAND AND WALES,

Delivered to the SOCIETY, the FRIENDS of the PEOPLE, affociated for the Purpofe of obtaining a PARLIAMENTARY REFORM, on Saturday the 9th of February 1793.

LONDON:

PRINTED, BY ORDER OF THE SOCIETY, FOR D. STUART, NO. 52, FRITH-STREET, SOHO ; AND SOLD BY ALL THE BOOKSELLERS IN TOWN AND COUNTRY.

TO THE SOCIETY,

THE FRIENDS OF THE PEOPLE,

ASSOCIATED FOR THE PURPOSE OF OBTAINING

A PARLIAMENTARY REFORM.

REPORT of the COMMITTEE appointed to Report upon the State of the Reprefentation in England and Wales.

YOUR COMMITTEE apprehend that they cannot better comply with the intentions of your Society, than by arranging the fubject referred to them under diftinct Heads, and giving a plain ftatement of facts unmixed with any argumentative inference, and accompanied by no other obfervations than fuch as a due attention to perfpicuity may appear to render neceffary.

To this line of proceeding your Committee feel more particularly attached, becaufe it carries with it that internal evidence of opennefs and fair dealing which muft conciliate the unprejudiced, even if it were poffible it fhould fail to convince them, and confines the opponents of reform to that iffue which fets at defiance all fpeculation and fophiftry, and on which every man is capable of forming a judgment. An unembellifhed detail of facts muft, to be refuted, be invalidated; and for the fame reafon that it is impregnable if well founded, it is eafily fhaken if buiit on falfhood or error. By the very plan of their Report, therefore, your Committee give an unequivocal teftimony that they reft their claim to credit folely upon the accuracy of their ftatements; and they offer a fubftantial proof that they fear no inveftigation into what they advance, by the manner in which they advance it.

Your

Your Committee have confidered the flate of the reprefentation under three general Heads :—

First. They have examined into THE REPRESENTATION AS IT EXISTS IN POINT OF FORM ;

And herein,

1ft. *Of the divifion of the reprefentation*, or the proportions in which the different counties of England contribute to the total number of reprefentatives.

2dly. *Of the diftribution of the elective franchife*, or the proportional number of voters by which the different reprefentatives are elected.

3dly. *Of the right of voting*, or the various reftrictions and limitations under which the privilege of a vote for the choice of a reprefentative is beftowed.

4thly. *Of the qualifications to be poffeffed by candidates, and thofe elected*—and

5thly. *Of the duration of Parliaments.*

Secondly. They have examined into THE MODE IN WHICH ELECTIONS ARE CONDUCTED AND DECIDED ;

And herein,

1ft. *Of the length of time to which polls are protracted, and the caufes thereof.*

2dly. *Of the expence and inconvenience arifing from the diftance between the refidence of the elector, and the place of election.*

3dly. *Of the influence of corporations by the powers intrufted to the returning officers.*

4thly. *Of the appeal to the Houfe of Commons under the operations of the Acts, 10th, 11th, 25th, and 28th of Geo. III. as far as the fame relate to expence and delay.*

Thirdly. They have fhewn THE MISCHIEF RESULTING FROM THE DEFECTS AND ABUSES POINTED OUT IN THEIR REPORT ;

And herein,

Of the fyftem of PRIVATE PATRONAGE, and the influence poffeffed by Peers and wealthy Commoners, in the nomination of what are called the Reprefentatives of the People.

By this divifion of the fubject your Committee exhibit a view of reprefentation, confidered with refpect to *its component parts, the mode in which thofe parts are combined,* and the *confequences and effects of the whole fyftem.*

YOUR Committee find that the number of reprefentatives is 513 (exclufive of Scotland), and that they are returned to ferve in Parliament by the different counties in the following proportions to the grofs number :—

Of the divifion of the reprefen- tation, or the proportions in which the dif- ferent counties of England con- tribute to the total number of reprefentatives.

40 Counties return 2 each,	—	—	80
12 Counties (Wales) 1 each,	—	—	12
			—— 92

Thefe Counties, which are claffed according to the ufual divifion of England, return Members for the different Cities, Towns, and Boroughs they contain, in the following proportions, viz.

Northern Counties.

Northumberland, including Berwick,	—	—	6
Cumberland,	—	—	—	—	4
Weftmoreland,	—	—	—	—	2
Durham,	—	—	—	—	2
Yorkfhire,	—	—	—	—	28
Lancafhire,	—	—	—	—	12
Northern Counties return, exclufive of County Members,			—— 54

Middle Counties Weftward.

Chefhire,	—	—	—	2
Derbyfhire,	—	—	—	2
Staffordfhire,	—	—	—	8
Warwickfhire,	—	—	—	4
Worcefterfhire,	—	—	—	7
Shropfhire,	—	—	—	10
Herefordfhire,	—	—	—	6
Monmouthfhire,	—	—	—	1
Gloucefterfhire,	—	—	—	6
Middle Counties Weftward return, exclufive of County Members,			—— 46

Carry over   ——192

Middle

Middle Counties Eastward.

		Brought forward	— 192
Oxfordshire,	— — — —	5
Buckinghamshire,	— — — —	12
Bedfordshire,	— — — —	2
Northamptonshire,	— — — —	7
Nottinghamshire	— — — —	6
Rutland,	— — — —	0
Leicestershire,	— — — —	2
Lincolnshire,	— — — —	10
Huntingdonshire,	— — —	2

Middle Counties Eastward return, exclusive of County Members, — 46

Eastern Counties.

Norfolk,	— — — —	10
Suffolk,	— — — —	14
Cambridgeshire,	— — — —	2
Hertfordshire,	— — —	4
Middlesex,	— — — —	6
Essex,	— — — —	6

Eastern Counties return, exclusive of County Members, — 42

Western Counties.

Dorsetshire,	— — — —	18
Somersetshire,	— — — —	16
Devonshire,	— — — —	24
Cornwall,	— — — —	42

Western Counties return, exclusive of County Members, — 100

Southern Counties.

Kent,	— — — —	8
Suffex,	— — — —	18
Surrey	— — — —	12
Hampshire,	— — — —	24
Berkshire,	— — — —	7
Wiltshire,	— — — —	32
Cinque Ports,	— —	16

Southern Counties and *Cinque Ports* return, exclusive of County Members, — 117

12 *Counties* of *Wales* return 1 each, exclusive of County Members, 12

2 *Univerſities,* 2 each, — — — 4

Total 513

Your

Your Committee, having thus fhewn the proportions in which the different counties and divifions of England are reprefented, will next endeavour to point out *in what proportions the elective franchife is diftributed among the body of electors.*

Your Committee have found it impracticable to obtain any accurate account of the total number of electors in England, but they conceive that the neceffity for fuch an account is effentially obviated by the one which they are enabled to lay before you. The following ftatement, on the general correctnefs of which they can rely, is conclufive to prove, that, by the partial and unequal manner in which the mafs of electors is divided, fuch a proportion of the 513 reprefentatives is returned to Parliament by a few, as renders it of little confequence by how many the remainder is elected. If 3 perfons be chofen by 30, and 2 by 4970, though undoubtedly the 5 are chofen by 5000 ftill it will hardly be contended that fuch a diftribution of the electors does not effectually take away every advantage of popular reprefentation.

Your Committee find that *two hundred and fifty-feven Members*, being a *majority* of the Commons of England, are elected by 11,075 *voters;* or in other words by little more than the 170th *part* of the People to be reprefented, even fuppofing them to be only *two millions.*

The operation of this defect in the reprefentation cannot however be thoroughly underftood, without obferving the manner in which the body who return this majority is *fub-divided;* for this purpofe your Committee have drawn out the following ftatement, in order to bring before you in detail, the number of electors by which each of the different Reprefentatives, who conftitute a majority of the Houfe of Commons, is chofen; and, with a view to fhew all that the reprefentation even pretends to be, your Committee have confidered *Burgage* tenures, and other rights of a fimilar defcription, as creating *real* voters; the actual number of which they have taken into their calculation, reckoning them as electors having individually a free choice.

A STATEMENT

OF

The Proportions, in which the Elective Franchife is diftributed among that Body of Electors who return the Majority of the 513 Members for England and Wales.

Places where the right of Voting is in Burgage and other Tenures of a fimilar Defcription.				Number of Voters	Members
	Number of Voters	Members	Beaumaris -	24	2
			Bewdley -	14	1
Appleby -	220	2	Bifhop's Caftle -	50	2
Afhburton -	200	2	Bodmyn -	36	2
Great Bedwin -	80	2	Bofliney -	20	2
Beeralfton -	100	2	Brackley -	33	2
Blechingly -	90	2	Buckingham -	13	2
Boroughbridge -	74	2	Calne -	34	2
Bramber -	36	2	Camelford -	19	2
Clitheroe -	102	2	Caftle Rifing -	50	2
Cockermouth -	260	2	Chriftchurch -	40	2
Downton -	20	2	Corff Caftle -	20	2
E. Grinftead -	36	2	Devizes -	30	2
Heytefbury -	50	2	Droitwich -	14	2
Horfham -	60	2	Dunwich -	40	2
Knarefborough -	110	2	Eaft Looe -	20	2
Malton -	200	2	Edmondfbury -	36	2
Midhurft -	100	2	Gatton -	10	2
Northallerton -	200	2	St. Germains -	20	2
Petersfield -	154	2	Grampound -	50	2
Richmond -	270	2	Harwich -	31	2
Rippon -	186	2	Helfton -	36	2
Ryegate -	200	2	Haftings -	12	2
Saltafh -	38	2	Launcefton -	20	2
Old Sarum -	7	2	Lifkeard -	50	2
Thirfke -	50	2	Leftwithiel -	24	2
Weobly -	45	2	Lyme Regis -	31	2
Weftbury -	50	2	Lymington -	18	2
			Malmefbury -	13	2
Electors	2938 return	52	Marlborough -	7	2
			St. Mawes -	36	2
			St. Michael -	42	2
Places where the Number of Voters does not exceed 50.			Newport (Hants) -	24	2
Alborough (Suffolk)	35	2	Newtown (Lancafhire)	50	2
Andover -	15	2	Newtown (Hants)	36	2
Banbury -	19	1	Orford -	20	2
Bath -	32	2	Romney -	13	2

Number

	Number of Voters	Members		Number of Voters	Members
Rye -	15	2	Bridport -	180	2
Scarborough -	44	2	Chippenham -	140	2
Taviftock -	50	2	Cambridge -	200	2
Thetford -	31	2	Dorchefter -	200	2
Tiverton -	26	2	Eye -	200	2
Truro -	26	2	Guildford -	120	2
Wilton -	50	2	Heydon -	190	2
Winchelfea -	9	2	Hindon -	200	2
Wycombe -	48	2	Huntingdon -	200	2
Yarmouth (Hants)	13	2	Ilchefter -	150	2
			St. Ives -	180	2
Electors	1449	return 100	Ludgerfhall -	110	2
			Minehead -	160	2

Places where the Number of Voters does not exceed 100.

			Milbourne Port -	114	2
Agmondefham -	70	2	Morpeth -	200	2
Aldborough (Yorkfhire)	57	2	Penryn -	140	2
Callington -	62	2	Plymouth -	160	2
Dartmouth -	98	2	Plympton -	104	2
Weft Looe -	70	2	Queenfborough -	131	2
Fowey -	63	2	Retford -	112	2
Great Grimfby -	75	2	Wallingford -	140	2
Haflemere -	60	2	Wareham -	150	2
Higham Ferrers -	84	2	Wendover -	120	2
Hythe -	96	2	Woodftock -	200	2
Montgomery -	80	1	Wootton Baffet -	160	2
Newport (Cornwall)	62	2	Winchefter -	110	2
Oakhampton -	96	2			
Poole -	100	2	Electors	4461	return 56
Portfmouth -	60	2			
Salifbury -	54	2			
Seaford -	82	2	*Places where the Number of Voters does not exceed 300.*		
Steyning -	100	2	Marlow -	216	2
Stockbridge -	102	2	Bridgewater -	230	2
Totnefs -	80	2		446	4
Tregony -	60	2			
Wenlock -	100	2	ABSTRACT.		
Whitchurch -	70	2	2,938	elect	52

Of the different rights of voting, or the various limitation &re-ftrictions, under which the privi-lege of voting is beftowed.

YOUR COMMITTEE will now call your attention to *the various rights of voting* which are exercifed in the different places returning members to Parliament.

They find that the members for the 52 counties are all elected by one uniform right. Every man throughout England, poffeffed of 40 fhillings per annum freehold, except in certain cities and towns having peculiar jurifdictions, is entitled to a vote for the county in which fuch freehold is fituated.

With refpect to the different cities, towns, and boroughs, they exercife a variety of feparate and diftinct rights, fcarcely capable of being claffed in any methodical order, and ftill lefs of being afcertained by the application of any fixed principle. In the greater part of them indeed the right of voting appears to be vefted in the *freemen of bodies corporate*, but, under this general defcription, an infinite diverfity of peculiar cuftoms is to be found. In fome places the number of voters is limited to a felect body not exceeding 30 or 40 ; in others it is extended to 8, or 10,000. In fome places the freeman muft be a refident inhabitant to entitle him to vote ; in others his prefence is only required at an election. The right to the freedom is alfo different in different boroughs, and may, according to the peculiar ufage, be obtained by birth, fervitude, marriage, redemption, &c. &c.

The remaining rights of voting are of a ftill more complicated defcription. Burgageholds, leafeholds, and freeholds,—fcot and lot, inhabitants houfeholders, inhabitants at large, potwallopers, and commonalty, each in different Boroughs prevail, and create endlefs mifunderftandings and litigation, from the difficulty which is daily found to arife in defining and fettling the legal import of thofe numerous diftinctions, which, in fome places, commit the choice of two members to as many inhabitants as every houfe can contain ; in others, to the poffeffor of a fpot of ground where neither houfes nor inhabitants have been feen for years, and which, in a few inftances, have even prevented the wifdom of Parliament from finally determining who are entitled to vote, or what the right is *.

YOUR

* Pomfret, Poole, Weftminfter, Ludgerfhall, Newark, and Carlifle, have appeals upon the right of voting before the Houfe of Commons remaining yet undecided.

A great variety of cafes might be quoted to fhew the inconvenience arifing from the prefent complicated rights of voting ; that of *Saltafh* in particular is too curious to be unnoticed. Since the year 1772, it has occupied the attention of no lefs than *five Committees*, and is ftill open to difpute. In 1785, the right was determined to be in the *corporation*, and the candidates returned by them were declared to be duly elected. One of thefe gentlemen having vacated his feat, a new election brought the queftion again before the Houfe, when the right was determined to be in the *burgage holders*, and the feat given accordingly.

Your Committee have not entered into any detail of the different rights of voting, becaufe it would have extended their report to a very tedious, and, in their opinion, a very unneceffary length ; they cannot however pafs over this part of their enquiry without calling your attention to the following facts, conceiving that the manner in which the voice of the people is at prefent collected, cannot be placed in a ftronger point of view by ftating thofe who *are*, than by defcribing fome of thofe who *are not* entitled to vote.

A man poffeffed of 1000*l. per annum, or any greater fum, arifing from copyhold, leafehold for* 99 *years, trade, property in the national funds, or even freehold in the city of London, and many other cities and towns having peculiar jurifdictions* *, *is not thereby entitled to vote.* -

Religious opinions create an incapacity to exercife the Elective Franchife. All *Catholics* are excluded generally, and by the operation of the Teft Laws, *Proteftant Diffenters* are deprived of a voice in the election of Reprefentatives in about thirty boroughs, where the right of voting is confined to the corporate officers alone.

A man paying taxes to any amount, how great foever, for his domeftic eftablifhment, does not obtain a right to vote unlefs his refidence be in fome borough where that right is vefted in the inhabitants. To afcertain how far this exception applies, your Committee have carefully examined into the number of boroughs in which the elective franchife is committed to the inhabitants, and they find them to be 60, of which 28 contain lefs than 300 voters. Your Committee muft here add, that it appears by a return made to Parliament, from the Tax-office, in 1785, that the number of houfes paying taxes was 714,911.

SUCH appears to be the nature of the principal qualifications, and reftrictions under which the right of voting is beftowed or withheld ; it next remains to be fhewn *who may legally be chofen as the reprefentative.*

Your Committee find a variety of difabilities created by different ftatutes, or the cuftom of Parliament. By thefe, minors, papifts, aliens, clergymen in prieft's orders, fheriffs, and other returning officers in their refpective jurifdictions, perfons concerned in the management of certain duties, or poffeffing certain offices, contractors, and perfons holding penfions during pleafure, are incapa-

accordingly. By thefe contradictory decifions two gentlemen voted in Parliament for three years, cach of them denying the pretenfions of the other, and the Houfe of Commons having at different times decided againft the right of both.

For a competent knowledge of the various rights of voting, fee the *Reports* of Meffrs. *Douglas, Luders, Phillips,* and *Frazer*, where, in nine volumes, much light is thrown upon the fubject.

* *At Kingfton upon Hull*, for inftance, the number of freeholders, thus excluded, is ftated to amount to 500.

citated

citated to fit in the Houfe of Commons. Befide thefe difqualifications, there is alfo another moft material one, by which the Electors are precluded from making choice of any man not poffeffed of property *in land*. By the 9th. Anne, c. 5. every Candidate, if required, muft take an oath that he has a clear eftate of freehold or * copyhold, to the value of 600l. per annum in the cafe of the Knight of a Shire, and 300l. in the cafe of a Citizen or Burgefs; and the oath muft be renewed when the member takes his feat. The only exception is in favour of the reprefentatives of the two Univerfities, and the eldeft fons or heirs apparent of peers, and perfons poffeffing 600l. per ann. from whom no qualification is required.   .

WITH refpect to *the duration of Parliaments*, your Committee find, that by an act paffed in the year 1694, (or foon after the Revolution), it was declared, that, " *By the ancient laws and ftatutes of this kingdom, frequent parliaments ought to be held, and that frequent and new Parliaments tend very much to the happy union and good agreement of the King and People,*" and therefore it was enacted, " *that no parliament fhould laft longer than for three years.*"

In the firft year of the reign of Geo. I. (or 1715) the Parliament, which was thus elected for *three* years, determined that it would be more convenient to hold their feats for *feven*, and by a law at that time paffed, and ftill unrepealed, fuch at prefent is the legal term, before the expiration of which the people cannot revoke their truft, be the conduct of their reprefentatives what it may. The royal prerogative gives however to the King a better fecurity for the good behaviour of the Commons toward the Crown, by enabling him to diffolve the Parliament at any hour which to his Minifters fhall feem proper.

---

* A Copyhold qualifies to *reprefent*, but not to *elect*.

OF THE MODE OF CONDUCTING ELECTIONS.

Your Committee having reported upon the various heads which the first division of their enquiry prefented to them, and having, in fo doing, laid before you what may be called the conftituent parts of an election, (namely, the places entitled to fend reprefentatives, who are qualified to choofe, and who to be chofen) come next to examine in what manner thofe different rights are brought into action, and to ftate to you, *the mode in which Elections are conducted.*

Your Committee find that election proceedings are carried on with extreme inconvenience to the electors, and exceffive expence to the candidates. The two evils are however fo intimately blended, and depend fo much upon each other, that, from an idea that a feparate and diftinct difcuffion of them would only lead to tirefome repetition, and unneceffary detail, it has been thought moft advifeable, to confider them both under one head.

The firft defect in the fyftem eftablifhed for collecting the opinions of the People, to which your Committee will requeft your attention, is, that the *Poll*, whether the voters confift of 10, or 10,000, and whether the right of voting be in inhabitants refident, or in freemen, or freeholders difperfed throughout the county, is *only taken in one fixed place* [*]. A freeholder of *Cornwall*, living in *Northumberland*, muft forego the exercife of his franchife, or travel to *Leftwithiel*; and a freeman of *Berwick* refiding at *Falmouth*, can only be heard as an Elector after a journey of 400 miles.

As thefe may be called extreme cafes, and your Committee are above all things anxious to confine themfelves within the limits of ftrict fact and practice, they conceive it neceffary to enter into fome detail on this fubject.

In county elections it frequently happens that the freeholder, living in the county itfelf, muft go 40, 50, or 60 miles before he can be admitted to poll ; but thefe are trifling journies compared to what muft be taken by thofe who, being freemen of one city or town, refide in another. Your Committee have thought they could not furnifh better information refpecting this inconvenience, than by confulting and making extracts from a certain number of thofe poll books, which are printed at different Boroughs by authority of the returning officer, and which diftinguifh the number of *refident* from *non-refident* freemen. From thefe it appears that, at the following places, the proportion at the laft contefts ftood thus :

* Except in *Hampfhire*, where, for " the cafe of the inhabitants," the Sheriff has a power of removing the Poll to the Ifle of Wight. 7 & 8 W. 3. c. 25. f. 10.

Canterbury

	Refidents	From London	From the Country	Total
Canterbury -	832	153	354	1339
Coventry -	1891	356	278	2525
Bedford -	919	187	332	1438
Lincoln - -	428	126	406	960
Newcaftle (Northumberland)	1148	208	889	2245
Briftol - -	3957	663	1429	6049
Colchefter -	528	227	525	1280
Lancafter -	657	144	1481	2182

From the above, which are fclected from a great variety of fimilar inftances, to give a general idea of the fubject, it appears, that in many places the non-refident are nearly equal to the refident voters, and in fome places actually out number them.

Your Committee have not thought it neceffary to ftate more than two claffes of non-refidents, viz. thofe *from London*, and thofe *from the country* generally. The variety of diftances from which the latter are brought, would, if here fet down, extend this Report to too great length, but the curious may eafily fatisfy them-felves by a reference to the printed poll-books. Your Committee conceive they give an average fufficiently correct, when they take the diftance which the country voters have, one with another, to travel, to be, for each place, *a fourth part* of the diftance which fuch place is from London. Thus the non-refident country voters for Briftol, it is to be affumed refide 30 miles from the place of poll, thofe living in London not being nearer than 120 miles.

On enquiry among thofe agents who have been in the habit of managing the conveyance of voters from one place to another, fuch accounts have been re-ceived of the extravagant expence attending this part of an election as would, if here fet down, fubject your Committee to the imputation of having exaggerated in their ftatement. For inftance, every voter at *Newcaftle upon Tyne*, coming from London, is faid to coft 30l.; at *Exeter* 20l.; at *Briftol* 15l.; at *Colchefter* 10l. The reafons affigned for fuch exorbitant charges are, that the greater part of the free-men are tradefmen, or mechanics, who cannot be fuppofed to travel great dif-tances, merely for the fake of giving a vote; that they are to be enticed from home, if not by direct bribery, at leaft by the inducement of pleafant convey-ance, good accommodations, and reafonable fatisfaction, if not fome thing more, for their trouble and lofs of time; and that, when a candidate undertakes to pay the travelling expences of a man who is to confer a favour upon him at the end of the journey, it cannot be expected that he will venture to fcrutinize too clofely into the expedition with which he proceeds, or the length of the bills he incurs on the road.

What

What effect this reasoning may have on the minds of those who are not conversant in Elections, your Committee know not; but the accuracy of the following *Estimate*, which, for the better understanding the extent of the expence in question, they have thought it proper to lay before you, will not, they persuade themselves, be controverted, except for the purpose of adding to the amount.

Estimate of the least Expence of conveying a Voter from the Place of his Residence to the Place of the Poll.

Sixpence per mile—cost of conveyance.
Seven shillings and Sixpence per day—cost of maintenance.
Ten shillings and Sixpence per day—for loss of time and trouble.

This * last charge is calculated from the sum which, on an average, is paid on the same account to witnesses from the country attending Election Committees in the House of Commons.

According to this estimate it appears, that

A voter taken 50 miles to poll, will cost,

		£		
For conveyance out and home	-	2	10	0
For three days maintenance	- -	1	2	6
For three days loss of time and trouble	-	1	11	6
		£5	4	0

A voter taken 250 miles to poll, will cost,

For conveyance out and home	-	12	10	0
For seven days maintenance	-	2	12	6
For seven days loss of time and trouble	-	3	13	6
		£18	16	0

In the above, your Committee have supposed that the voter spends only *one clear day* at the place of election; but they must observe, that, from every information they have been able to collect, his stay there is generally much longer.

* It is true, that in the strictness of the law, the voter is not entitled to be paid for his loss of time and trouble, but the practice of doing it has become so general, and the propriety of it so universally assented to, that it is now notoriously insisted upon by all voters, and necessarily complied with by all candidates.

With

With refpect to the expedition with which the voter travels, it is impoffible to lay down any fixed rule as to the number of miles to be travelled in one day; but your Committee apprehend, they may be fairly ftated to be from 50 to 90, according to the diftance of the entire journey. A voter, for inftance, would be a day in going from London to Canterbury (56 miles) and probably not more in going to Coventry (91 miles); and in fuch‘ journeys as from London to Newcaftle (273 miles) he might continue to travel at the rate of 80 or 90.

If any credit be given to‘the accuracy of thefe eftimates, it will be eafy, with the affiftance of the preceding extracts from the printed poll-books, to form an idea what the expence of bringing non-refident voters to poll muft be in places where the electors are numerous.—Thus,

At Colchefter.—The voters refident in London, being 227, to be brought 50 miles to poll, muft, if abfent 3 days, coft at leaft 5l. 4s. each, or altogether, - - £.1180

At Coventry.—The voters refident in London, being 356, to be brought 90 miles, fuppofing them only to be out ‘3 days, coft 7l. 4s. each, or altogether, - - £.2563

At Newcaftle upon Tyne.—The voters refident in London, being 208, to be brought 274 miles, muft, fuppofing them to be abfent from home 7 days, coft at leaft 20l. each, or altogether, - - - - £.4160

At Briftol.—The voters refident in London being 663, to be brought 120 miles, even fuppofing them only to be out 4 days, muft coft at leaft 9l. 12s. each, or altogether, £.6364

The non-refident voters coming from the different parts of the country, your Committee have before propofed to confider as travelling one quarter of the diftance which the place of election is from London; but as it would be difficult to lay down any fixed rule by which to eftimate the length of time the country voters are abfent from home, they will leave every perfon to form his own calculation on this branch of expence. The truth is, that where the diftance is under 25 miles, fome voters will go and return in one day, whereas others, where the diftance is above 10 miles, will make their polling a bufinefs of two days. Much depends on the voters character and occupation. If, however, the country voters belonging to Briftol were to be eftimated as cofting only 2l. 8s. each (that is reckoning them to be abfent only one day,) they would altogether be a charge upon the candidates of 3,429l.; which, added to the

expence

expence of London voters, would make *the total amount to be defrayed, for non-refident electors* 9,793¹.

This evil of the voters refiding at a place diftant from the poll has alfo another effect, namely, the rendering nugatory an act paffed *to prevent giving meat and liquor at elections.* Cuftom has fanctioned the propriety of opening public houfes for the reception of voters from the country, and it may eafily be conceived how impoffible it muft be, during the tumult of an election, to diftinguifh one defcription of electors from another; the confequence is, that the refident freemen are equally with the non-refidents admitted to participate in the diftribution of liquor, and that the whole town is a fcene of drunkennefs and confufion, to the great inconvenience of the inhabitants, and the intolerable expence of the candidates.

Your Committee know not in what way they can bring before you any exact detail of the various other expences to which candidates are liable. A heavy charge is incurred from the fees payable on the admiffion of freemen having an inchoate right; that is, a right acquired, but not claimed, and which, as it is to be exercifed for the benefit of the candidate, is fo generally taken up at his expence, that from cuftom it is never confidered as an act of bribery. Thefe fees vary much, and amount from five fhillings to five guineas for each admiffion. The numerous points of law which arife in the courfe of every conteft make it neceffary for the parties to have the affiftance of counfel, and folicitors; the manœuvres which attend all polls, conducted upon a fyftem of fuch intricacy as they are at this day, require the exertions of many vigilant agents; the very cockades form an indifpenfable and heavy coft in an election; nor can any candidate, fpeaking generally, flatter himfelf with much hope of fuccefs, unlefs his liberality and contempt of economy keep equal pace with the extravagance of his competitor. All thefe however are evils which thofe, who have never been concerned in elections, cannot perhaps be made to feel, and which to thofe, who are converfant in them, will appear much under-rated. Your Committee proceed in their report of thofe inconveniences which admit of direct proof, and the next to which they muft turn is—

The extreme length to which Polls are protracted.

It has been fhewn that be the number of voters what it may, the poll is to be taken in one fixed place;—it is now to be feen how long that place is liable to be expofed to the dreadful tumult, diforders, and outrages which are but too well known to attend election contefts.

By an act paffed in the 25th *Geo.* 3. *c.* 84. (1785) for " the better regulation of polls and fcrutinies," the continuance of polls is authorized to laft during *fifteen days.*

Of the reasons which induced the Legislature to acknowledge the propriety of so very tedious a proceeding, your Committee can give no account, but they will endeavour to explain the nature of the methods practised to fill up the number of days thus liberally allowed. They must not however here omit to remark, that by the 11th *Geo.* 1. *c.* 18. (unrepealed by the statute above quoted) the poll for *the city of London* must be closed within *seven* days from its commencement; a limitation the more extraordinary, as the voters in the city of London amount to a number not exceeded by any place in England, except Westminster.

If a candidate wish to procrastinate, he has several ways open to him by which he may protract the poll to the utmost extent of its legal limits.

He may direct his friends to vote one by one as slowly as possible. By a custom, which from practice has obtained the force of a law, a poll cannot be closed unless no vote be tendered within a reasonable time after the returning officer has made three proclamations. By having a vote therefore ready to tender after every second proclamation, a candidate may continue to protract the business of the poll to such a length as may tend to the infinite vexation and expence of his antagonist.

But should it happen that he, whose interest it is to delay, has not friends enough at hand to *feed the poll*, (as it is called) in the above manner, the law provides him with another mode of carrying his point. He may require all the *oaths* to be actually administered which certain statutes authorize him to insist upon. These are in number no less than six, viz. the oath of *Allegiance*, the oath of *Supremacy*, the *Bribery Oath*, the oath of *Residence*, the *Declaration of Test*, and the oath of *Abjuration*. The act of giving a single vote may thus be converted into a tedious and troublesome operation.

Should neither of the beforementioned expedients be thought sufficient, there still remains a never-failing source of procrastination in the complicated and ill-ascertained qualifications and disqualifications of electors. Dull indeed must be the counsel who attend an election, if in the way of objection or reply they cannot contrive to lengthen the proceedings to the utmost extent of their client's wishes.

the powers
vested to the
rning Offi- YOUR COMMITTEE come now to speak of *the power entrusted to the returning officer*, and which, in fact, in all corporate towns, is the power of the select body who choose him.

Of the various means of influence and corruption thrown into the hands of these select bodies by the present system of elections, your Committee could speak

largely

largely did they not fear the detail would be too extensive for the limits of their report. They therefore make no comments upon the number of civic honours, and employments, with which these formidable bodies can tempt the ambition, or the interests of the opulent; they forbear to observe upon the controul they obtain over the lower class of people, by the terrors of their magisterial authority; they say nothing of the influence derived from the power of granting or refusing licenses, from the discretion with which they are frequently invested in the distribution of public charities, or the weight they possess from the appointment of parish officers, and the superintendance of poor rates, and parochial assessments; —your Committee in this place will only call your attention to the power they enjoy through the medium of *the returning officer.*

The returning officer is vested with the entire and uncontrouled superintendance of whatever relates to the conduct of an Election. He is entrusted with absolute authority from the hour of his receiving the precept, to the hour in which he makes his return; for the law reposes the most unbounded confidence in his wisdom and his honesty, as will be seen by the following statement of the various discretionary powers committed to him.

When he receives the precept from the sheriff, he is to make proclamation of the day of election; and *this he may,* without assigning any reason for so doing, *bring on either on the 5th, 6th, 7th, or 8th day,* as to him may seem good to enlarge or curtail the notice. A variety of cases may readily be conceived in which this power of expediting or protracting might be of infinite importance to the interests of the candidates, but your Committee will only mention two, viz. Where freemen have been made by redemption or purchase, and want a few days to compleat the twelve months, before the expiration of which, they cannot legally vote; or, where the right being in inhabitants householders, or persons paying scot and lot, some of them have not finished the six months residence which the statute requires as necessary to constitute an inhabitant.

When the day of election is fixed, *the returning officer is to appoint the poll clerks;* and the encreasing or reducing the number of these, tends, in populous places, materially to expedite or retard the proceedings.

During the time of the election *the returning officer has the peace of the borough under his care,* and he may, at his discretion, create as many assistant constables as he may choose to think there is occasion for;—these he will scarcely select but from among those who are in the same interest with himself.

But though he is thus empowered to provide for the preservation of the peace, *the existence of tumults and riots gives him a fresh opportunity of exercising his discretion.* By the 25 of Geo. III. it is enacted, that the poll must be kept open a certain number of hours in every day, " unless prevented by *any un-*

D   *avoidable*

avoidable accident." What is " an unavoidable accident," the returning officer is to decide ; fo that the whole operation of this provifion of the law is left to his difcretion. Particularly it refts with him to determine, in the event of any *difturbance*, whether it require an adjournment, and for *how long*.

But the great fource from which a returning officer derives his confequence and power, remains yet to be ftated.

Hitherto your Committee have only fpoken of duties which require no more than honeft intentions to difcharge properly ;—they now come to confider a truft repofed in him, for the due execution of which not only integrity, but peculiar difcernment, penetration, and legal ability are abfolutely neceffary.

The extreme importance annexed to the proper difcharge of the duties of which your Committee are now about to fpeak, cannot be better explained than by examining into the precautions taken by the legiflature on another occafion of precifely the fame nature.

A trial of the merits of an election before a Committee of the Houfe of Commons, is no more than *a repetition of the trial had before the returning-officer* at the time of the poll. The points in difcuffion are the fame ; and the regulations thought neceffary by Parliament for the inveftigation of them upon the appeal, abundantly prove the intricacies in which the prefent fyftem of election laws are involved, and the ftrong temptations to which the judgments of thofe who are to decide, are virtually acknowledged to be expofed.

To enquire into the merits of a petition complaining of an undue return of a member to ferve in Parliament, when the queftion is brought before the Houfe of Commons, it is thought neceffary to fecure impartiality by choofing a jury of thirteen by ballot ; and to prevent the inconvenience that would arife if the lot fhould fall on thirteen gentlemen, unaccuftomed to judicial proceedings, the Parties are permitted to nominate two more, who are added to them.

With fuch caution is it thought neceffary to conftitute the Court, which, *upon the appeal*, is to enquire into the difputed rights of voting, the qualifications, and difqualificat ons of electors, and the various legal diftinctions which arife from the operation of fo extenfive a body of ftatutes as thofe relative to elections. The Committee fo appointed have alfo full power to fend for perfons, papers, and records, and to examine witneffes upon oath.

At the Election itfelf the fame truft is committed to *one man*, who, though originally only a *miniflerial* officer, is vefted with equal authority to decide, but left to form that decifion from the mere affertions of partial witneffes not fpeaking upon oath, and to oppofe whofe teftimony, whatever he may fufpect, or either party demand, he can neither compel the attendance of perfons, nor the production of written evidence. All difputable points of law which arife in the courfe of an
Election,

Election, are fubmitted to his *fole* determination. *He* is to fettle what fhall or fhall not be received as evidence, and arbitrarily to decide upon all doubtful votes which he may admit, or reject at his pleafure. In a word, to his *uncontrouled judgment*, and to the *purity of his motives* in the exercife of it, the Houfe of Commons looks for the legal and true Reprefentative of the People.

The magnitude of the truft, and the corrupt practices of which thofe who pof-fefs it are to be fufpected, your Committee apprehend they have fufficiently fhewn, by ftating *the jealoufy with which the Legiflature delegates it to its own Members.* Why they fhould difplay fo much lefs anxiety for wifdom and inte-grity in the taking of the original poll than in its revifion, your Committee do not prefume to guefs, but a due attention to facts compels them to affert, that it cannot be from any reafonable prepoffeffion in favour of Returning Officers, becaufe your Committee muft report them to be, very frequently *notorioufly illi-terate and needy*; very generally *avowed partizans of one of the candidates*; and almoft always *appointed by intrigue or cabal*. Of the numerous petitions pre-fented to Parliament, there is fcarcely one but what contains fome charge againft them either for *partiality* or *corruption*; and of the various mal-practices in which they have been detected, and of the multitude of offences of which they have been convicted, let the Journals of Parliament, from the firft volume to the laft, bear teftimony.

YOUR COMMITTEE having thus explained the manner in which Elections are conducted, come now to ftate *the nature of the remedy provided by the Legiflature, in all cafes where the propriety of the Return is difputed.*

There are various Statutes exifting, upon which actions may be brought againft Returning Officers wilfully neglecting their duty, or making falfe returns; but as thefe only *give damages*, and do not *affect the feat in Parliament*, your Com-mittee conceive it unneceffary here to recapitulate them, and therefore proceed immediately to the very celebrated remedy introduced in the 10th year of his Majefty's Reign, and commonly known by the name of *Mr. Grenville's Act.*

The operation of this appeal, of late years fo much extolled, your Committee are under the painful neceffity of declaring to be a fource of *vexatious delay* and *intolerable expence*; and they call the following facts to confirm their affertion.

The laft General Election took place in the month of June 1790, and the Petitions prefented to Parliament, complaining of undue Returns, were in Number 39 [*]; of thefe *twenty-one* were decided *within twelve months*; *nine more within two years*, and the opening of the year 1793 has feen the Houfe of Commons with difficulty

[*] See the Votes of the Houfe of Commons.

procure

procure Committees to proceed upon the complaints of the remainder. It is to be obferved, that the perfons returned, *exercife*, till the Petitions againft them are brought to a hearing, *every privilege of a Member of Parliament*; and it has happened, that men have fat in the Houfe, and voted during the two laft Seffions of the prefent Parliament, without, as it has afterwards appeared, having had any pretenfions whatever, beyond the good wifhes of a pliant Returning Officer. The event of the Petitions, now depending, may poffibly fhew, that fome even fit three Seffions (or *one half of the ufual duration of a Parliament's exiftence*) with as little right on their fide.

Such is the manner in which the Houfe of Commons poftpones the decifion of the Appeals brought before it. When at laft the fuitors have the fortune to procure a hearing, the length to which the proceedings are protracted exceeds all bounds. The Court can only fpare time to fit five hours in each day, and the number of days which may be confumed in the trial of a Petition, will appear from the following account of the duration of fome of thofe which have been tried within thefe laft ten years †.

		Committee appointed	Report made		Trial lafted Days
1784	Downton	17th January	19th July	-	32
1784	Ivelchefter	29th June	21ft July	-	22
1785	Bedford county	18th March	19th May	-	62
1785	Cricklade	14th February	4th April	-	49
1785	Downton	17th February	9th March	-	20
1785	Penryn	24th February	18th March	-	22
1785	Southwark	3d March	4th April	-	32
1786	Seaford	22d February	13th March	-	19
1787	Norwich	15th February	9th March	-	22
1789	Colchefter	26th February	6th April	-	39
1789	Weftminfter	3d April	6th July	-	95
1791	Carlifle	25th February	14th March	-	17
1791	Exeter	4th March	23d March	-	19
1791	Ludgerfhall	29th March	14th April	-	17
1791	Oakhampton	3d February	28th February	-	25
1791	Fowey	8th February	7th March	-	27
1791	Steyning	15th February	7th March	-	20
1791	Downton	7th April	17th May	-	40
1791	Newcaftle (Staffordfh.)	23d February	21ft March	-	26
1792	Horfham	16th February	10th March	-	22
1792	Steyning	13th March	5th April	-	23
1792	Seaford	28th February	19th March	-	19
1792	Cirencefter	5th March	10th May	-	66

† See the Votes of the Houfe of Commons.

Your

YOUR COMMITTEE having thus shewn the *delay* and *inconvenience* to which they who apply for redress to the House of Commons, are exposed, have only to state the *expence* to which they are likewise subjected, in order that a thorough knowledge may be had of the situation in which Petitioners are placed, who appeal from the decision of the returning officer.

Your Committee might lay before you numerous accounts, and those perfectly authentic, of the enormous sums expended by parties having petitions tried before the House of Commons, but, always preferring to quote those facts which are easiest to be proved, they will only avail themselves of the particular cases where the charges have been recorded.

By the 28th *Geo*. III. where petitions are reported to have been frivolous and vexatious, *taxed costs are allowed*; by referring therefore to those petitions which have been so reported, your Committee are enabled, from authority, to give a general idea of the expences attending an appeal to the House of Commons. They only beg it may be remembered, that the amounts stated underneath, are the *taxed*, and not the *real* costs, which they understand to have been nearly double, and that they are the charges defrayed by only *one* of the parties.

The hearing of the petition for *Barnstaple* lasted 8 days—taxed costs £ 514

1791	*Westminster*	2 days	-	-	396
1791	*Colchester*	2 days	-	-	463
1791	*Launder*	2 days	-	-	240
1791	*Orkney*	3 days	-	-	198
1791	*Bodmyn*	1 day	-	-	

YOUR COMMITTEE will sum up all that has been said respecting the mode of conducting elections, and the operations of Mr. Grenville's acts, by a plain narrative of the progress of two recent contests. The *first* at *Seaford*, where the number of voters is less than 90; the *second* at *Westminster*, the most populous borough in England.

At *Seaford*, the object of one of the candidates was to protract the election till twenty-six of his friends had completed the fix months residence, which the law requires to constitute inhabitancy, and of which term, when the dissolution of Parliament took place in June 1790, *seventeen days* were wanting.

The means adopted on the occasion to obviate this difficulty, were attended with success. The returning officer was cautious, and patient. Exercising his discretionary power to the utmost extent, he did not bring on the election till the *eighth day** after receiving the precept, and the remaining *nine days* were con-

---

* In 1784 the returning officer for Seaford chose to be as much expeditious in his proceedings as in 1790 he was too dilatory. He brought on the election on the *fourth*; the consequence of which was, that it was determined to have been *void*, and the parties were exposed to the expence of a second contest.

fumed in purfuing the methods mentioned in the former part of this Report. The qualifications and difqualifications of the voters were canvaffed at full length, and their principles and purity examined by the teft of every oath which the law has at any period invented againft Popery, bribery, &c.—The Counfel argued, the returning officer doubted, the candidate harangued, and the electors fwore, till the neceffary number of days were paft, which qualified the twenty-fix new inhabitants to vote. The poll then clofed, and the candidate, whofe intereft it had been to procraftinate, carried his point, merely by manœuvre and delay.

The lofing candidate prefented a petition to the Houfe of Commons againft this return, but could not obtain a hearing *till the 28th of February,* 1792. A committee was then appointed, which after fitting *nineteen* days, reported to the Houfe on the 19th of March, that the member returned was not duly elected, and that his opponent was entitled to the feat—*a feat, of which he had been illegally deprived for near two years, becaufe the returning officer required nine days to poll lefs than ninety votes, and the recovery of which was attended with an expence perfectly incompatible with every idea of free reprefentation.*

The *fecond* cafe to which your Committee beg your attention, relates to *Weftminfter.*

The election came on the 18th of July, 1788, and the poll continued 14 days. A petition was prefented to Parliament, complaining of an undue return, and it came to a hearing on the 3d of April, 1789.

The Committee continued to fit till the 18th of June, when they came to the following moft extraordinary refolutions.

Refolved, " That from the progrefs which the Committee have hitherto been " enabled to make, fince the commencement of their proceedings, as well as " from an attentive confideration of the different circumftances relating to the " caufe, a final decifion of the bufinefs before them cannot take place in the " courfe of the prefent feffion, and that NOT IMPROBABLY THE WHOLE OF THE " PRESENT PARLIAMENT MAY BE CONSUMED IN A TEDIOUS AND EXPENSIVE " LITIGATION.

Refolved, " That from the neceffary length of the proceeding, and the ap-" proach of a General Election, which muft occur not later than Spring 1791, " (*nearly two years diftant*) THE PROSECUTION OF THE CAUSE ON THE PART OF " THE PETITIONERS PROMISES TO BE FRUITLESS, AS FAR AS IT RESPECTS THE " REPRESENTATION OF WESTMINSTER IN THE PRESENT PARLIAMENT.

Refolved, " That it be recommended to the petitioners to withdraw their " petition under the fpecial circumftances of the cafe."

The

The bufinefs, however, proceeded till the 6th of July, when *the petitioner was obliged to relinquifh his claim, after in vain attempting to bring it to a final iffue in the courfe of a hearing which lafted* ABOVE THREE MONTHS.

In all this long period, the only act of the Committee which bore even the appearance of a judicial decifion, was a refolution refpecting *the right of voting in Weftminfter.* Againft this determination an appeal was prefented to the Houfe of Commons on behalf of the electors, in July 1789, and, though regularly renewed in every feffion, has not yet been favoured with a hearing, notwithftanding it has been before the Houfe *above three years.* The confequence is, that *at this hour the right of voting in Weftminfter remains unfettled,* and fhould another conteft take place, it would again expofe the candidates to a tedious, expenfive, and probably fruitlefs litigation.

YOUR COMMITTEE conceive they cannot better conclude this part of their enquiry than by a fhort ftatement of the general refults which arife from it;
They therefore report, that it appears,

That, the number of reprefentatives affigned to the different counties is grofsly difproportioned to their comparative extent, population, and trade.

That, a majority of what are called the reprefentatives of the Commons are returned by the 170th part of the male fubjects of England paying taxes, even fuppofing thefe only to amount to two millions.

That, the partial diftribution of the elective franchife, which fubdivides this 170th part into 155 other parts, commits the choice of reprefentatives to felect bodies of men of fuch limited numbers, as renders them an eafy prey to the artful, or a ready purchafe to the wealthy.

That the right of voting is regulated by no uniform or rational principle refpecting either property or condition. That from the caprice with which it has been varied, and the obfcurity in which it has become involved by time and contradictory decifions, it is a fource of infinite confufion, litigation, and expence.

That the manner in which elections are conducted is difgraceful to the name of free election. That it is inconvenient to the elector, and ruinous to the candidate. That it is a fcourge to the honeft and peaceable, and a harveft to the diffolute and corrupt.

That the power given to returning officers, too often, (except in counties) men of extreme ignorance, or known depravity, added to the delay of the Houfe of Commons in attending to the petitions for redrefs, frequently deprives the electors of their true reprefentative for years.

The

val.

That the prefent fyftem of election laws which profeffes to qualify a man for Parliament who poffeffes three hundred pounds a year, is only calculated to infult the People with the fhew of an independent choice, becaufe, by its operation, it difables all, who have not incomes of at leaft as many thoufands, from becoming candidates.

Laftly, *That* the length of the duration of Parliaments, fubjected to the will of the Crown, tends to make the reprefentative independent of the conftituent, to render him fubmiffive to the commands of thofe in power, and to difturb " that happy union and good agreement between the King and People," which, by our anceftors at the Revolution, was fo conftitutionally afferted to arife " from " frequent and new elections."

OF PRIVATE PATRONAGE, AND THE INFLUENCE POSSESSED BY PEERS AND COMMONERS.

YOUR COMMITTEE having explained the nature of the representation confidered with refpect to its feparate and diftinct parts, having fhewn the defective and inconvenient materials of which it is compofed, and pointed out the difficulties thereby thrown in the way of the fair elector and the independent candidate, come now to invelligate the operation of the whole, and to examine and report what is the general refult as it affects the fecurity of the Conflitution, and the liberties of the country at large.

Your Committee are aware, that, in fpeaking upon this head, they are about to enter on a fubject which they might eafily difcover many inducements to pafs over in filence ; but they feel that they have undertaken a public duty of an importance which precludes all idea of liftening to any private confiderations, and they eagerly embrace the opportunity of proving their fincerity in the caufe of the people, by a full, an explicit, and an impartial ftatement.

To this line of conduct, even if they were not urged by principle, they would be compelled by motives of regard for the character of that Society to which they have the honor to belong. Such unprecedented pains have been taken to difcredit the intentions with which you have profeffed to act ; fuch high and unexpected authorities have been exerted to hold you up rather as the enemies than the Friends of the People, that your Committee conceive it their duty, to enable you to join iffue with your calumniators, and, prepared with every evidence the caufe requires, to appeal to the fober judgment of the country.

YOUR Committee report, that the grofs defects and abufes which, under the preceding heads, they have proved to exift in the prefent mode of reprefentation, have eftablifhed A SYSTEM OF PRIVATE PATRONAGE, which renders the condition of the Houfe of Commons *practically* as follows.

71 Peers and the Treafury nominate	-		90
Procure the return of	-	-	77
Patronage of 71 Peers and the Treafury			167
91 Commoners nominate	-	-	82
Procure the return of	-	-	57
Patronage of 91 Commoners	-	-	139
162 return	-	-	-	306 out of 513 Members.

E

The

This statement your Committee are aware will create confiderable furprize; and as many may be taught to doubt its accuracy, they have thought it neceffary to explain the nature of their calculation, and on what it is founded, in fuch a manner, as that every man may be enabled to correct their errors, if they have erred, or to convince himfelf of the truth of what they have afferted.

With this view they have given the names of the different Patrons, and are happy that thofe names are of too refpectable a defcription to afford the moft remote fufpicion that any invidious motives have produced the mention of them.

The Patronage your Committee have divided under two heads—*Nomination*, and *Influence*; and attributed it to diftinct perfons, under the defcriptions of *Peers* and *Commoners*.

With refpect to this firft divifion, your Committee defire to have it underftood that,

By a *nomination*, they would defcribe that *abfolute authority in a borough which enables the patron to command the return.* The number of places fet down in this clafs might, your Committee have every reafon to believe, be with ftrict propriety confiderably encreafed, but from a wifh to avoid all cavil, they have confined themfelves to fuch boroughs as are under undoubted controul. Thefe, in general, are the private property of the patrons, or have the right of voting vefted in a fmall corporate body, the majority of whom are his immediate dependents.

By *Influence*, your Committee would defcribe *that degree of weight acquired in a particular county, city, or borough, which accuftoms the electors on all vacancies to expect the recommendation of a candidate by the patron, and induces them, either from fear, from private intereft, or from incapacity to oppofe, becaufe he is fo recommended, to adopt him.*

This diftinction between Nominations and Influence has appeared neceffary for feveral reafons. It is true that the effect of both is nearly alike, but ftill it might feem improper to fpeak of them in the fame terms. The reprefentation of *Old Sarum* and of *Chefter* could not, for inftance, without much offence, be claffed under the fame head, and there are many other places, where, though the will of the patron is conftantly *complied with*, it would perhaps feem too harfh a phrafe to fay that he can *command*.

On the fubject of the *counties*, which are ftated to be under influence, your Committee are efpecially anxious to fay a word or two in explanation.

THEY would be forry that, owing to any mifapprehenfion, it fhould be conceived that in every inftance where they ufe the word *influence*, an injurious fonfe fhould be annexed to it. Property, they well know, will always have a
confiderable

confiderable operation, nor is it meant to infinuate that, becaufe there is faid to be influence, corruption muft neceffarily be fuppofed to exift. Where fortune enables, and difpofition induces a man to difcharge the friendly offices of neighbourhood and connexion with zeal and liberality, your Committee would be deeply concerned to be fufpected of a wifh to arraign, or in any manner decry the extenfive and honorable attachment which fuch a line of conduct muft, and ought to procure.

Property may however obtain a degree of weight beyond what is natural to it. It may be enabled to excite fear as well as to procure refpect; and without purchafing a majority, or controuling its dependents, it may acquire fuch power as to overcome and bear down all oppofition.

Precifely this fpecies of power is thrown into the hands of the wealthy, by the fyftem on which at this day elections are conducted. It confines the choice of the electors within the ranks of opulence, becaufe, though it cannot make riches the fole object of their affection and confidence, it can and does throw obftacles almoft infurmountable in the way of every man who is not rich, and thereby fecures to a felect few the capability of becoming candidates.

This monopoly has not however been obtained without many and vigorous ftruggles, but it has unfortunately happened that refiftance has but ferved to tighten the cord. Contefts have been found to be attended with fuch extravagance, party heat, tumult, expence, and litigation, and the dreadful effects of thefe have fpread fo wide and endured fo long, that, on the profpect of a vacancy, more confideration is now beftowed to contrive the means of *preferving the peace of the county*, (the phrafe ufed on thefe occafions) than to fecure its freedom and independence.

The meafures adopted for this prefervation of the peace are different in different counties; in all, however, they are founded *on fome fort of* COMPROMISE, *by which a facrifice is made of at leaft one half of the Freeholders' Franchife.*

County Elections may be faid to be, in general, contefted, either *by two political Parties,* or *by two great families,* or *by a great family and the gentry.* In all thefe cafes the expedient ufually had recourfe to, to prevent the confequences of a ftruggle, is *for each of the contending interefts to name one member.*

Where political Parties alone are concerned, it cannot indeed be faid that fuch an arrangement comes under the head of influence or patronage, becaufe in truth its only operation is entirely to ftrike out of the reprefentation the county compromifed; but where *the conceffions are made from one great family to another,* or *from the gentry to a great family,* as is often avowedly the cafe, can there be a queftion as to the fituation in which at leaft one of the members returned by every county, fo circumftanced, is placed? *Does he not owe his feat to a Patron?* and is it in the power of the mafs of the freeholders to break the combinations thus formed against them, unless they shall have the very peculiar good fortune to find a man, who, with principles sufficiently independent to set him above the fear of offending those in power, is ready to incur the fatigues, and able to defray the enormous expence of a contest, conducted upon the gross system of abuse which has been explained by your Committee in the former part of their Report?

Much of what has here been said respecting the causes which contribute to bring the representation of counties within the reach of a patron's influence, applies to populous cities, and great towns: but in those there is also the additional influence to be stated which is obtained through the medium of the returning officer. From the strictest enquiries your Committee have been able to make, they are convinced that, in nine corporate towns out of ten, *one member, at least, is returned by the select body.* Of the fact the curious may easily inform themselves; but let it be remembered that, if it should be ascertained, the sole question will then be, who influences the select body?

It would have been an endless task to have discussed all the information your Committee have received respecting the probability of alterations in the state of the patronage at the next election, and as the whole of these suggestions are built on speculation, and whether well grounded or otherwise, *only change the name of the patron,* they have thought it best to confine themselves to what appears to have been the state of the various interests at the *last* general election.

With respect to the *influence of the Treasury,* your Committee apprehend that it will occasion much surprize to find it apparently so limited, but it must be observed, that this is not a species of influence subject to any direct proof, and therefore your Committee have, wherever they could, avoided the mention of it, by inserting the name of the ostensible patron, even where he openly holds a place during pleasure under government.

The sources whence the influence of the Treasury is derived in the five towns mentioned in the table, your Committee apprehend to be too notorious to require any explanation.

With regard to the distinction respecting *Peers* and *Commoners,* your Committee beg to be understood as having made it, because they have thought it their duty to point out the extent of an interference, which the House of Commons has uniformly declared to be unconstitutional.

At the commencement of every session, the following resolutions, are entered on the journals.

Resolved, " That no peer of this realm hath any right to give his vote in " the election of any member to serve in Parliament."

Resolved,

Refolved, " That it is a high infringement upon the liberties and privileges " of the Commons of Great Britain, for any Lord of Parliament, or any Lord " Lieutenant of any county, to concern themfelves in the elections of members to " ferve for the Commons in Parliament."

Your Committee have been the more difpofed to take notice of thefe refolutions, becaufe the power of the Houfe of Lords, in matters of election, has been prodigioufly encreafed within the laft ten years *by the creation of* NINE PEERS *who return, by nomination and influence, no lefs than* TWENTY-FOUR MEMBERS *to the Houfe of Commons.*—If, therefore, the interference of the Lords in the elections of the Commons be,, as the latter uniformly declare, a *high infringement* of their liberties and privileges, your Committee muft report thofe liberties and privileges to have been of late fubject to the moft alarming and frequent attacks.

Your Committee have thus endeavoured to explain the nature of the diftinctions they have made refpecting the patronage of the different places. Subject to thefe obfervations they proceed to lay before you the following table, and will only add the moft folemn affurance, that it is to the beft of their knowledge, a true and unexaggerated ftatement. If in any inftance they have erred by attributing a patronage to any nobleman or gentleman of which he is not poffeffed, let it be confidered whether, in correcting the miftake, you can do more than *eraſe one name for the purpofe of inferting another*, which, as no party fuggeftions ought here to have weight, cannot make any fubftantial difference. The object of your Committee is not to fhew that this or that particular fet of men have obtained the command of the reprefentation, but to prove that the *People have loft it* : If, therefore, they fhall even have committed fuch an error as to have put down any place in the table which is not only uninfluenced by the patron there named, but alfo uninfluenced by any fingle patron whatever, let it be examined, whether fuch place do not come under the defcription of being *compromifed by political parties*; if fo, it is equally taken away from the fervice of the People, though it cannot be faid to be given to the controul of an individual.

PATRONAGE OF PEERS.

S OF PATRONS.	NOMINATIONS.		INFLUENCE.	Total Members returned by Peers
nfdale _nominates_	1 for Appleby 2 - Cockermouth 2 - Haslemere	_influences_	2 for Westmoreland	7
nt Edgecumbe - -	1 - Bossiney 2 - Lestwithiel 2 - Plympton	—	1 - Fowey	6
t - - -	2 - Liskeard 2 - Grampound 2 - St. Germain's	—		6
Newcastle - -	2 - Boroughbridge 2 - Aldborough (Yorkshire)	—	1 - Newark 1 - East Retford	6
f Buckingham -	2 - Buckingham 2 - St. Mawes	—	1 - Buckinghamshire 1 - Aylesbury	6
sbury - -	2 - Marlborough 2 - Great Bedwin	—		4
Northumberland -	2 - Launceston 2 - Newport (Cornwall)	—		4
Marlborough - -	2 - Woodstock 1 - Heytesbury	—	1 - Oxfordshire 1 - Oxford	5
william - -	2 - Malton 1 - Higham Ferrers	—	2 - Peterborough	5
f Lansdowne - -	2 - Calne -	—	2 - Wycombe	4
ey - - -	1 - Whitchurch -	—	2 - Ludgershail	3
Devonshire - -	2 - Knaresborough -	—	1 - Derbyshire 1 - Derby	4
Bedford - - - -	2 - Tavistock -	—	1 - Bedfordshire 1 - Oakhampton	4
of Stafford - -	- - -	—	1 - Staffordshire 1 - Litchfield	4
tford - -	2 - Orford	—		2
ngdon - -	2 - Westbury	—		2
Norfolk - -	- - -	—	1 - Arundel	1
Rutland - -	1 - Bramber -	—	1 - Grantham 1 - Scarbro' 1 - Newark	4
Richmond - -	- - -	—	1 - Chichester 1 - Seaford	2
f Peers Patrons 19 nominate 50		influence 27	Total	77

NAMES OF PATRONS.		NOMINATIONS.		INFLUENCE.		
Brought forward 19	50		Brought forward 27			
Lord Radnor	-	nominates 2 - Downton -	influences 1 -	New Sarum		
Duke of Beaufort	-	- - • - -	— { 1 -	Monmouthshire		
			1 -	Monmouth		
			1 -	Gloucestershire		
Lord Sandwich	- - •	- - -	— { 1 -	Huntingdonshire		
			2 -	Huntingdon		
Marquis of Bath	- - -	2 - Weobly	- - —			
Lord Egremont	-	- 2 - Midhurst	—			
Lord Westmorland	-	- 2 - Lyme Regis	—			
Lord Cornwallis	-	- 2 - Eye	—			
Duke of Grafton	- - -	• - - -	— { 1 -	Bury		
			1 -	Thetford		
Duke of Dorset	-	- 2 - Grinstead	—			
Duke of Bridgewater		2 - Brackley	—			
Lord Beverley	-	- 2 - Beeralston	- —			
Lord Camelford	-	- 2 - Old Sarum	- —			
Lord Foley	-	- 2 - Droitwich	- — 1 -	Worcestershire		
Lord Bute	-	- 1 - Bossiney	- — 1 -	Cardiff		
Lord Portsmouth	- -	- -	— 1 -	Andover	-
Lord Orford	-	- 1 - Castle Rising	- —			
Lord Malmesbury	-	- 1 - Christchurch	- - —			
Lord Hardwicke	-	- 1 - Ryegate	- — 1 -	Cambridgeshire		
Lord Somers	-	- 1 - Ryegate	- - —			
Lord Townshend	-	- 1 - Tamworth	- - —			
Lord Harrowby	-	- 2 - Tiverton	- - —			
Lord Darlington	-	- 1 - Winchelsea	- - —			
Lord Bulkeley	-	- 1 - Beaumaris	- —		- -
Lord Powis	-	- 1 - Montgomery	- - —			
Duke of Bolton	-	- -	- — 1 -	Totness		
Lord Spencer	-	• -	- — { 1 -	Oakhampton		
			1 -	St. Alban's		
Lord Falmouth	-	- 2 - Truro	—			
Lord Thanet	-	- 1 - Appleby	—			
Lord Guildford		- 1 - Banbury	—			
Lord Camden	-	- -	- - — 1 -	Bath		
Lord Poulett	-	- - -	- - — 2 -	Bridgewater		
Lord Grosvenor	-	• - -	- - — 2 -	Chester		
Number of Peers Patrons 51 nominate 85			influence 48			1 or

	NOMINATIONS	INFLUENCE	Total Members returned by Peers
Brought forward 51	*5	Brought forward 48	133
Bathurst -	*nominated* - -	*influences* 1 - Cirencester	1
Shaftesbury - - -	- -	— 1 - Dorchester	1
Berkeley - - -	- -	— 1 - Gloucestershire	1
Brownlow - - -	- -	— 1 - Grantham	1
Pembroke - -	- 2 - Wilton	—	2
Oxford -	- - -	— { 1 - Radnorshire / 1 - New Radnor }	2
: of Manchester -	- - -	— 1 - Huntingdonshire	1
Pelham - -	- - -	— 1 - Lewes	1
: of Portland -	- -	- — 1 - Nottinghamshire	1
Uxbridge -	- 1 - Milbourne Port	— { 1 - Anglesea / 1 - Carnarvon }	3
Exeter - -	- - - -	— 2 - Stamford	1
Warwick - -	- - - -	— 2 - Warwick	2
Petre - -	- - - -	— 1 - Thetford	1
Clarendon - -	- - - -	— 1 - Wootton Bassett	1
Bolingbroke - -	- - - -	— 1 - Wootton Bassett	1
Carlisle - -	- - - -	— 2 - Morpeth	2
Onslow - -	- - - -	— 1 - Guildford	1
Walpole - -	- - - -	— 1 - Lynn	1
Grimston - -	- - - -	— 1 - St. Albans	1
: of Leeds - -	- - - -	— 1 - Penryn	1
mber of Peers Patrons 71	nominate 88	influence 72 Total	160
Treasury	*nominate* 2 for Queenborough	- - - -	1
:to - -	- - -	*influence* 1 for Dover -	1
:to - -	- - -	1 - Rochester	1
:to - -	- - -	1 - Plymouth	1
:to - g	- - -	2 for Windsor -	2
Peers and the Treasury nominate	90	influence 77 Total	167

PATRONAGE OF COMMONERS.

NAMES OF PATRONS.	NOMINATIONS.	INFLUENCE.
William Drake, Efq. *nominates*	2 for Agmondefham	*influences*
Lord Clive -	2 for Bifhops Caftle -	1 for Ludlow .
Rev. Mr. Holmes	{ 2 for Newport (Hants) - } { 1 for Yarmouth (Hants) - }	- 9
Sir J. St. Aubyn, Bart.	1 for Helftone -	- -
——— Rogers, Efq.	1 for Helftone -	- -
W. Pulteney, Efq.	- - -	{ 4 for Weymouth, &c. { 1 for Shrewfbury
R. Barwell, Efq. -	{ 2 for Tregony { 1 for Winchelfea }	- - -
P. C. Crefpigny, Efq.	2 for Aldborough (Suffolk)	- -
——— Trefufis, Efq.	{ 2 for Callington - { 1 for Afhburton - }	- -
Sir H. Bridgman, Bart.	- - -	{ 1 for Wenlock { 1 for Wigan -
J. Buller, Efq. -	{ 2 for Saltafh - { 2 for Weft Looe -	- - -
——— Buller, Efq. -	2 for Eaft Looe -	- - -
Sir Francis Buller, Bart.	- - -	1 for Totnefs -
Sir R. Clayton, Bart.	2 for Blechingly -	- - -
Sir T. Dundas, Bart.	2 for Richmond -	- - -
Sir E. Deering, Bart.	2 for Romney -	- - -
Sir T. Frankland, Bart.	2 for Thirfke -	- -
Sir H. Burrard, Bart.	2 for Lymington -	- -
Sir H. Calthorpe, Bart.	1 for Bramber -	1 for Hindon -
Sir F. Baffett, Bart.	- -	-{ 1 for St. Michael's { 1 for Penryn -
Sir J. Honeywood, Bart.	2 for Steyning -	- -
Sir F. Sykes, Bart.	- - -	2 for Wallingford
Sir J. Vanneck, Bart.	1 for Dunwich -	- -
Sir F. Barrington, Bart.	1 for Newtown (Hants) -	- -
Sir R. Worfley, Bart.	1 for Newtown (Hants) -	- -
Sir C. Hawkins, Bart.	- - -	1 for St. Michael's
Commoners Patrons 26	39	15

NAMES OF PATRONS.	NOMINATIONS.	INFLUENCE.
Brought forward 26	39	15
Sir R. Palke, Bart. *nominates* 1 for Afhburton	*influences* -	-
Sir G. Yonge, Bart.	- - -	1 for Honiton
Sir C. Davers, Bart.	- - -	1 for Bury
Sir S. Fludyer, Bart.	- - -	1 for Chippenham
Sir W. W. Wynne, Bart.	- - -	1 for Denbighfhire
Lord Weftcote	1 for Bewdley	- -
Lord Middleton	1 for Whitchurch	- -
Sir C. Gould Morgan -	-	1 for Brecon
W. Joliffe, Efq. -	2 for Petersfield	- -
J. Robinfon, Efq.	2 for Harwich	- -
—— Wilkins, Efq.	2 for Malmefbury	- -
R. Troward, Efq.	2 for Ilchefter	- -
W. Praed, Efq. -	-	2 for St. Ives
T. P. Leigh, Efq.	2 for Newtown (Lancafhire)	- -
W. C. Meddlycott, Efq.	1 for Milbourne Port	- -
J. Calcraft, Efq.	2 for Wareham	- -
J. B. Church, Efq.	2 for Wendover	- -
Lady Irwin -	2 for Horfham	- -
Mrs. Allanfon -	2 for Rippon	- -
Sir Jonathan Phillips	2 for Camelford	- -
Thomas Lifter, Efq.	1 for Clitheroe	- -
P. A. Curzon, Efq.	1 for Clitheroe	- -
John Mortlock, Efq. -	-	2 for Cambridge Town
C. Anderfon Pelham, Efq.	-	2 for Grimfby
J. F. Luttrell, Efq. -	-	2 for Minehead
B. Barne, Efq. -	1 for Dunwich	-
J. Bond, Efq. -	1 for Corfe Caftle	-
H. Bankes, Efq. -	1 for Corfe Caftle	
E. Lafcelles, Efq. -	1 for Northallerton	-
H. Pierce, Efq. -	1 for Northallerton	-
R. Ladbroke, Efq. -	1 for Gatton	-
W. Currie, Efq. -	1 for Gatton	-
W. P. Afhe A'Court, Efq.	1 for Heytefbury	-
B. Howard, Efq. -	1 for Caftle Rifing	-
George Hunt, Efq. -	1 for Bodmin	-
Lord Milford	-	1 for Haverfordweft
Commoners Patrons 62	75	29

NAMES OF PATRONS.	NOMINATIONS.	INFLUENCE.
Brought forward 62	75	29
C. Forefter, Efq. - -	*influences*	1 for Wenlock -
J. C. Jervoife, Efq. *nominates* 1 for Yarmouth (Hants)	-	- -
C. Sturt, Efq. - -	-	1 for Bridport -
G. Rofe, Efq. -	1 for Chriftchurch	- - -
W. Evelyn, Efq. -	-	- 1 for Hythe -
St. C. F. Radcliffe, Efq. -	-	- 1 for Hythe -
T. W. Coke, Efq. -	-	- 1 for Derby -
T. Anfon, Efq. -	-	- 1 for Litchfield -
W. Lee Antonie, Efq. -	-	- 1 for Marlow -
T. Williams, Efq. -	-	- 1 for Marlow -
R. Middleton, Efq. -	-	- 1 for Denbigh -
Philip Rafhleigh, Efq. -	-	- 1 for Fowey -
C. Tudway, Efq. -	-	- 1 for Wells -
J. Dawkins, Efq. -	-	- 1 for Chippenham -
H. Penton, Efq. -	-	- 1 for Winchefter -
R. Peel, Efq. -	1 for Tamworth	- - -
James Sutton, Efq. -	-	- 2 for Devizes -
—— Whitaker, Efq. -	-	- 2 for Shaftefbury -
Sir P. Burrell, Bart. -	-	- 1 for Bofton -
Jof. Iremonger, Efq. -	-	- 1 for Andover -
W. Beckford, Efq. -	-	- 1 for Hindon -
Sir J. Carter -	-	- 2 for Portfmouth -
E. Baftard, Efq. -	-	- 2 for Dartmouth -
Edward Milward, Efq. -	2 for Haftings	- - -
Thomas Lamb, Efq. -	2 for Rye	- - -
P. Stephens, Efq. -	-	- 1 for Sandwich -
Lord Mulgrave -	-	- 1 for Scarbro' -
R. Gamon, Efq. -	-	- 1 for Winchefter -
Right Hon. T. Harley -	-	- 1 for Leominfter -
Commoners 91 nominate 82		57 Total

In the preceding table your Committee have in some places stated only *one member* to be returned by influence. The following is the list of those places, exclusive of the counties represented in a similar manner.

Aylesbury,	Lewes,	Guildford,	Retford,
Chichester,	Arundel,	Dorchester,	Bridport,
Lynn,	Plymouth,	Seaford,	Shrewsbury,
Wells,	Boston,	Bath,	Honiton,
Cirencester,	Ludlow,	Leominster,	Rochester.
Dover,	Oxford,	Sandwich,	Salisbury
Bodmin			

Your Committee not being able to procure any authentic information respecting the disposition of the *second vote* in these places, have forborn to make any estimate of it. In a few instances (most probably in all the counties) there is reason to believe that it is exercised with a proper spirit of independence ; but in general it can hardly be supposed that those who obsequiously surrender one half of their privileges, will be very scrupulous in the disposal of what remains.

The following boroughs, viz. *Stockbridge, Heydon,* and *Barnstaple,* though under the management of no particular patron, must not however be passed over in silence. The number of voters in them all does not amount to 500; and though your Committee do not think it prudent to state the fort of influence which they are informed has most weight in these places, they conceive it right to mention their names separately, that others may determine how far the members they contribute, might with propriety be added to the list of those, with whose return to parliament the unbiassed suffrages of the people have little or no concern.

It remains only to say a few words on the number of places *compromised by political parties.*

It has been before observed, that these arrangements *are made frequent by the intolerable expence attending contests,* to avoid which an expedient is adopted, which, in its operation, effectually destroys every principle of *representation.* Your Committee here speak of those *compromises* which take place *between political parties,* and which are very distinct from those *between two contending patrons,* or *a patron and the electors.* In the latter cases, the compromise relates to *men,* in the former to *measures.* It is not impossible but that those who are returned *by the influence of a patron,* may, (though not the organ through which the electors might wish to speak) in delivering their own, deliver the sentiments

of

of the electors, but those who are *returned by a compromise of parties*, must, to be faithful to their separate trusts, counteract the political consequence of each other, and deprive the borough that sends them to Parliament, of all parliamentary weight. When two gentlemen honestly and conscientiously profess principles diametrically opposite, (for your Committee are perfuaded that each of the members of the places in question is honourably attached to his party, by the conviction that such attachment is beneficial to his country) can it be said that the Borough which is represented by both of them, is represented for the purposes of more than a turnpike, or a paving bill. Will it be contended that such a choice can arife from any other cause *than a dread of the consequences that would attend any attempt to ascertain the real sentiments of the majority of the electors?* Or can it be believed that men *voluntarily* make a sacrifice of one half of their franchise, and that too in such a way as to render the half they retain of no value?

Let it not be thought that your Committee wish to cast any imputation on the electors who submit to these compromises. They do not merit any, for, in truth, they adopt them on compulfion; neither, while such a majority is returned in the manner that has been shewn, is it of any material confequence how or by whom the minority is elected. It has been afked why *Manchester*, *Birmingham*, and other populous places, do not petition for leave to fend Members to Parliament, and their filence has, by the enemies to Reform, been conftrued into an argument in favour of the present ftate of the reprefentation; but furely thefe *compromises* afford at once a fatisfactory anfwer, when it is feen that the mode of conducting elections is fuch, as makes *Newcaftle, Briftol*, &c. more anxious to wave than to exercife their privileges.

The following is a lift of the places compromifed by political parties—Newcaftle upon Tyne—Briftol—Chefhire—Effex—York—Weftminfter—Leicefter—Maldon—Lancafhire—Gloucefter—Prefton—Cumberland—Herefordfhire, and Suffex.

It only remains for your Committee to give the grand refult of their whole enquiries, and which, if the facts on which they have relied fhall be found to have been well grounded, will appear in the following

GENERAL STATEMENT.

71 Peers, and the Treafury, return		167
91 Commoners return		139
162 Peers and Commoners, with the Treafury, return		306
100 Electors at Poole return		2
102 ———— Stockbridge		2
190 ———— Heydon		2
250 ———— Barnftaple		2
200 ———— Wigan		* 1
54 ———— Salifhury		1
36 ———— Bodmyn		1
160 ———— Piymouth		1
200 ———— Bo on		1
83 ———— Seaford		1
32 ———— Bath		1
112 ———— E. Retford		1
180 ———— Bridport		1
120 ———— Guildford		1
240 ———— Lewes		1
190 ———— Arundel		1
200 ———— Dorchefter		1
17 Boroughs, not containing, on an average, 150 voters each, return		21
2611 Perfons, return to ferve in Parliament,	Members	327

To thefe 327 add 28, who are returned by *compromifes*, and it will appear, in what manner fuch a number of the Members of the Houfe of Commons is elected, as conftitutes a MAJORITY of no lefs than ONE HUNDRED AND NINETY-SEVEN of the Reprefentatives of England and Wales.

* Where only *one* member is ftated to be returned, it is to be underftood that the other has been accounted for under the head of Patronage.